This handwriting practice book belongs to :

_____

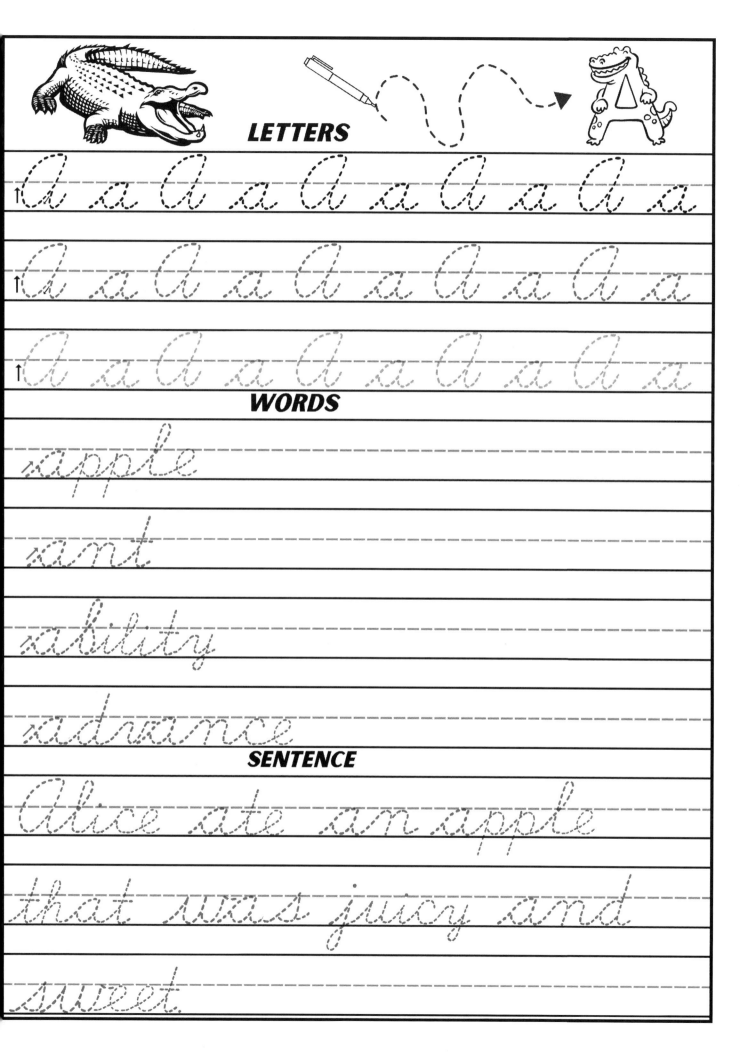

LETTERS

a a a a a a a a a

a a a a a a a a a

a a a a a a a a a

WORDS

apple

ant

ability

advance

SENTENCE

Alice ate an apple

that was juicy and

sweet.

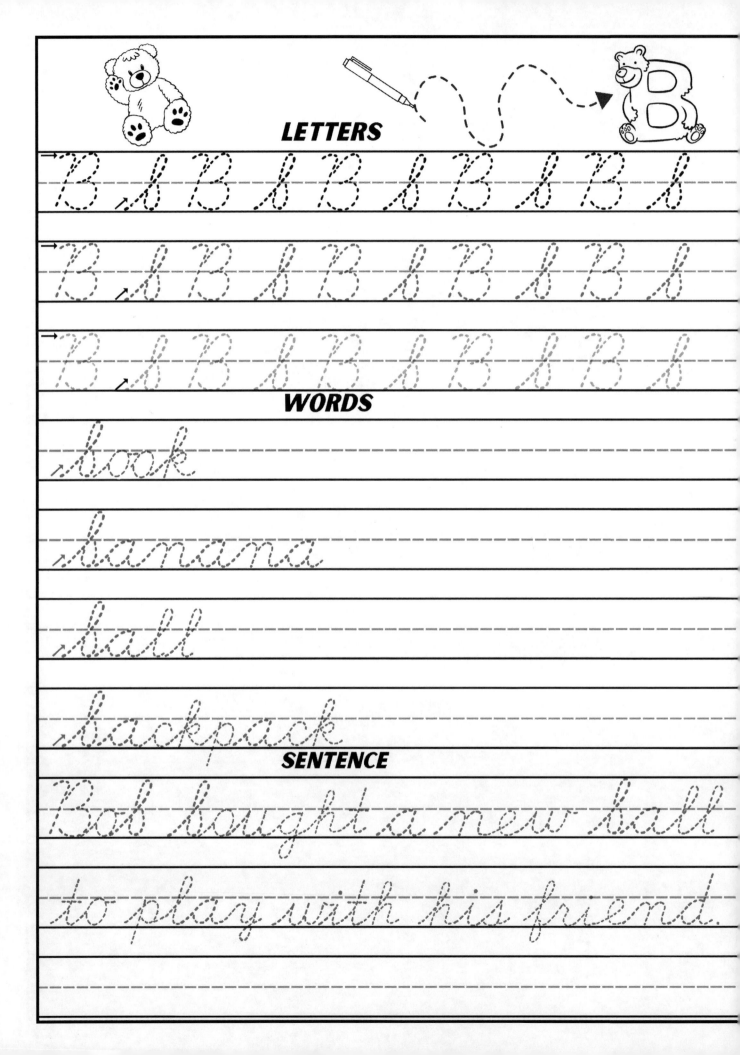

LETTERS

B B B B B B B B B B B B

B B B B B B B B B B B

B B B B B B B B B B B

WORDS

book

banana

ball

backpack

SENTENCE

Bob bought a new ball

to play with his friend.

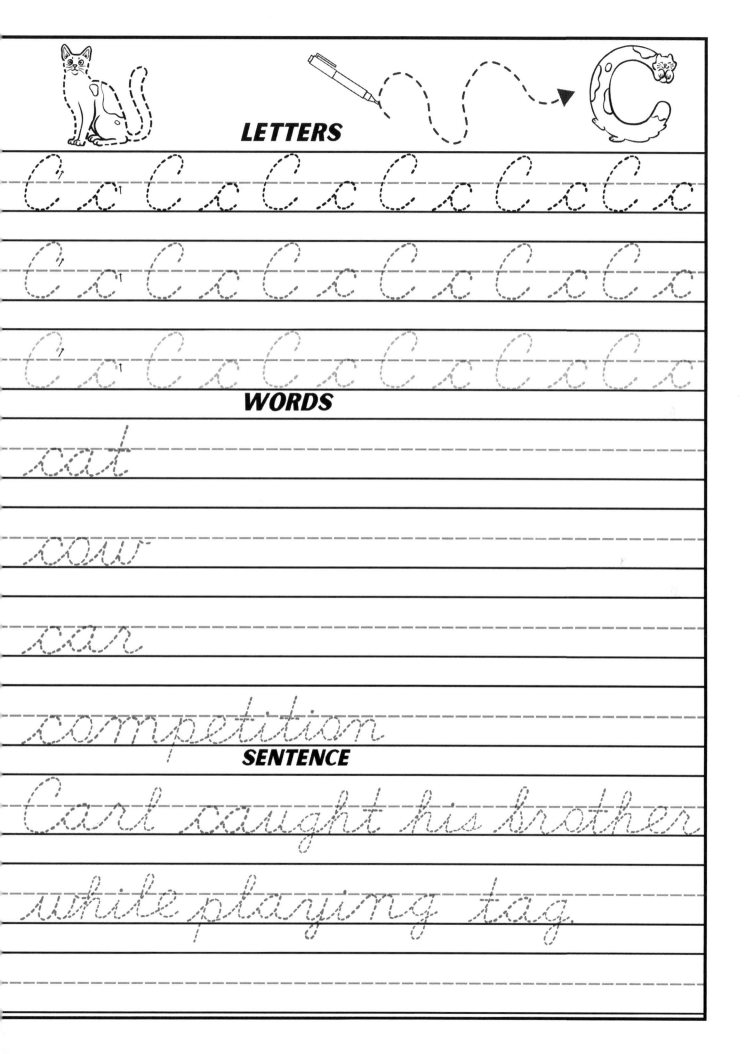

LETTERS

Cc Cc Cc Cc Cc Cc Cc Cc Cc

Cc Cc Cc Cc Cc Cc Cc Cc Cc

Cc Cc Cc Cc Cc Cc Cc Cc Cc

WORDS

cat

cow

car

competition

SENTENCE

Carl caught his brother

while playing tag.

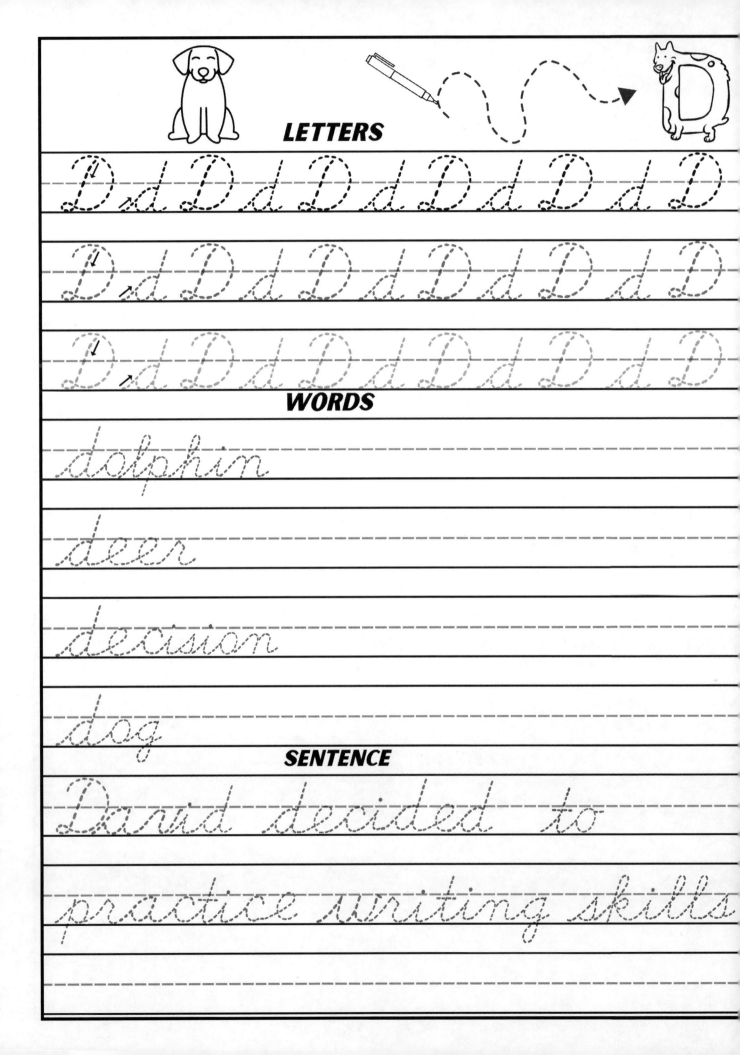

LETTERS

D d D d D d D d D d D d D d

D d D d D d D d D d D d D d

D d D d D d D d D d D d D d

WORDS

dolphin

deer

decision

dog

SENTENCE

David decided to

practice writing skills

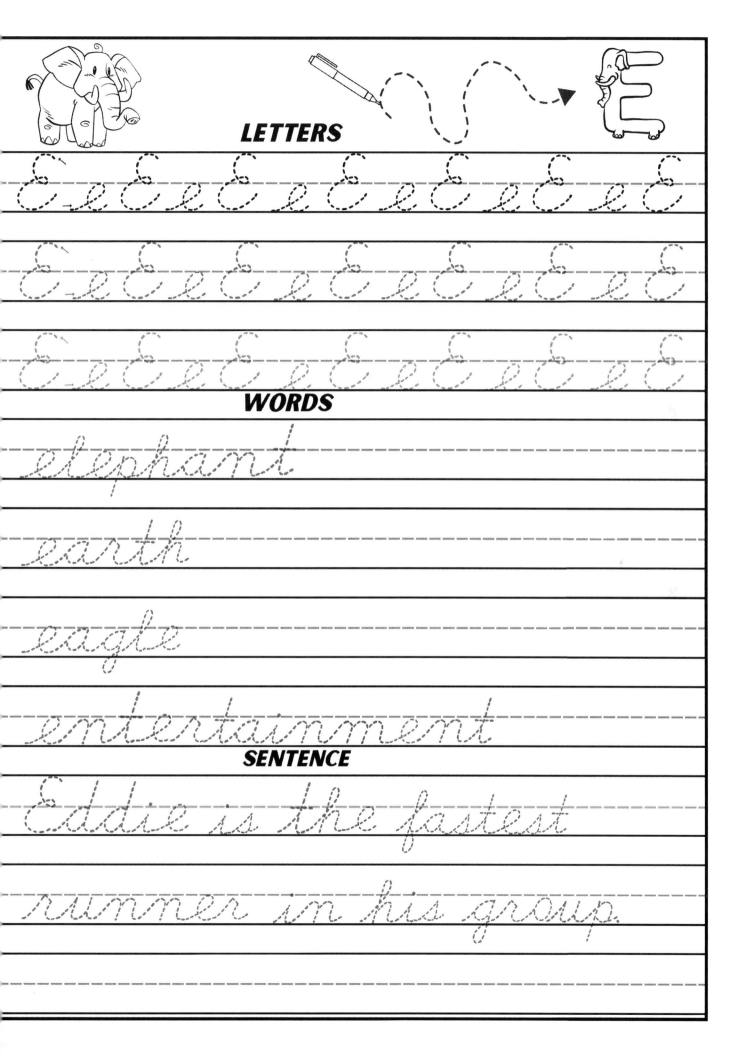

LETTERS

WORDS

elephant

earth

eagle

entertainment

SENTENCE

Eddie is the fastest

runner in his group.

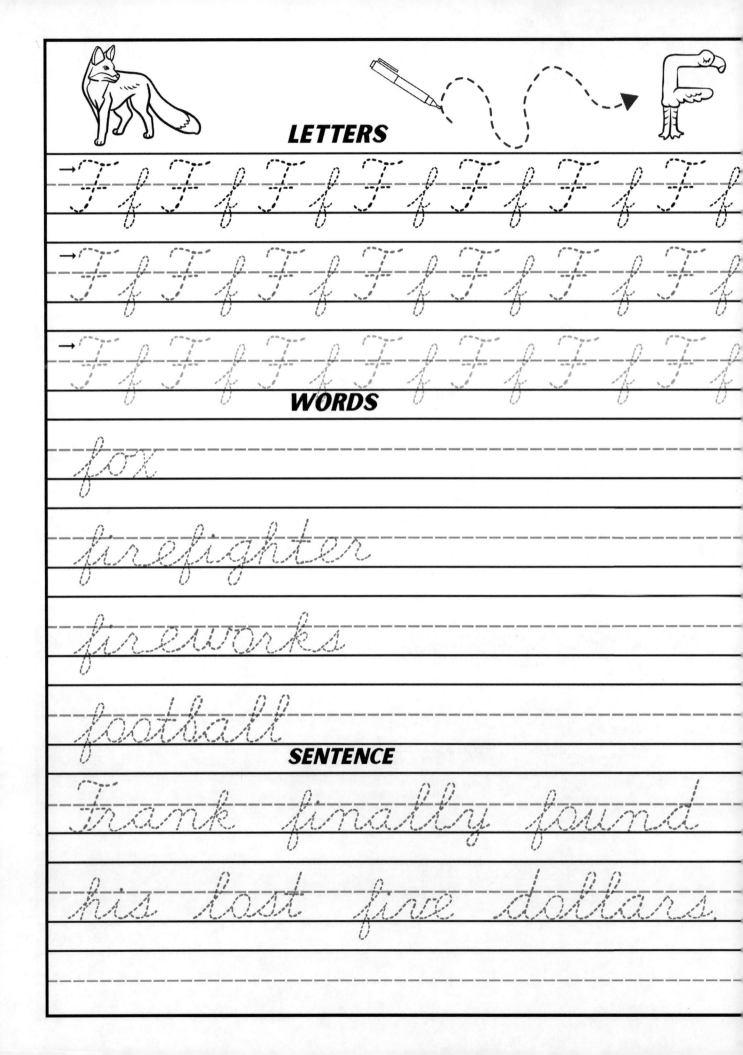

LETTERS

Ff Ff Ff Ff Ff Ff Ff Ff Ff

Ff Ff Ff Ff Ff Ff Ff Ff Ff

Ff Ff Ff Ff Ff Ff Ff Ff Ff

WORDS

fox

firefighter

fireworks

football

SENTENCE

Frank finally found

his last five dollars.

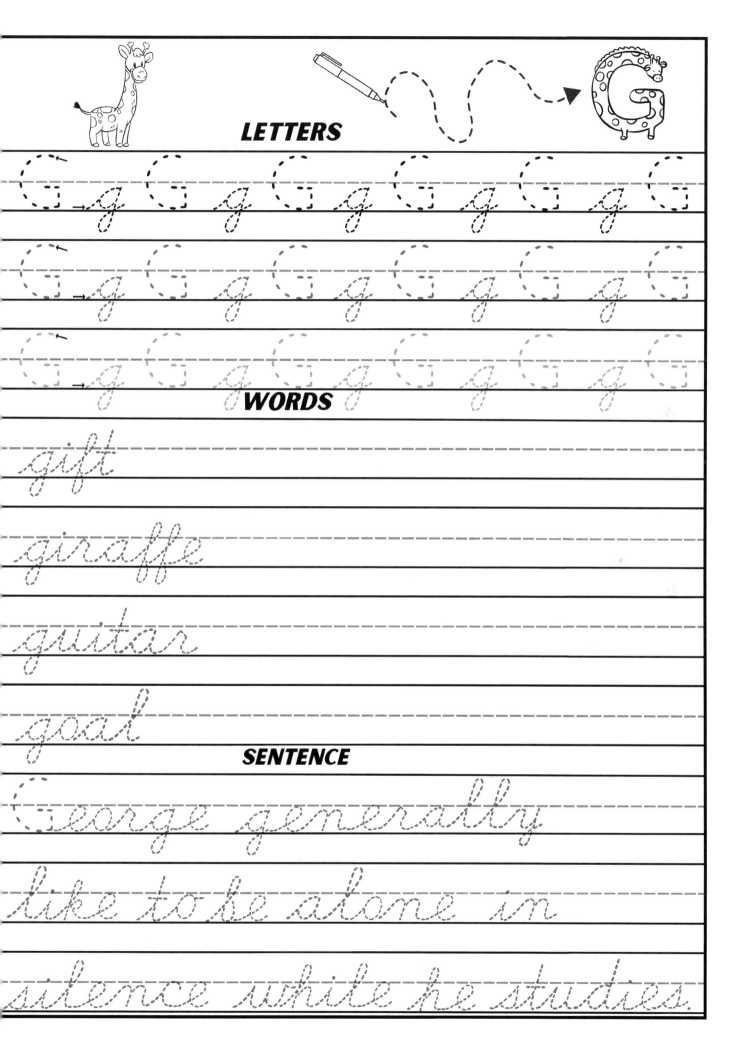

LETTERS

G g G g G g G g G g G

G g G g G g G g G g G

G g G g G g G g G g G

WORDS

gift

giraffe

guitar

goal

SENTENCE

George generally

like to be alone in

silence while he studies.

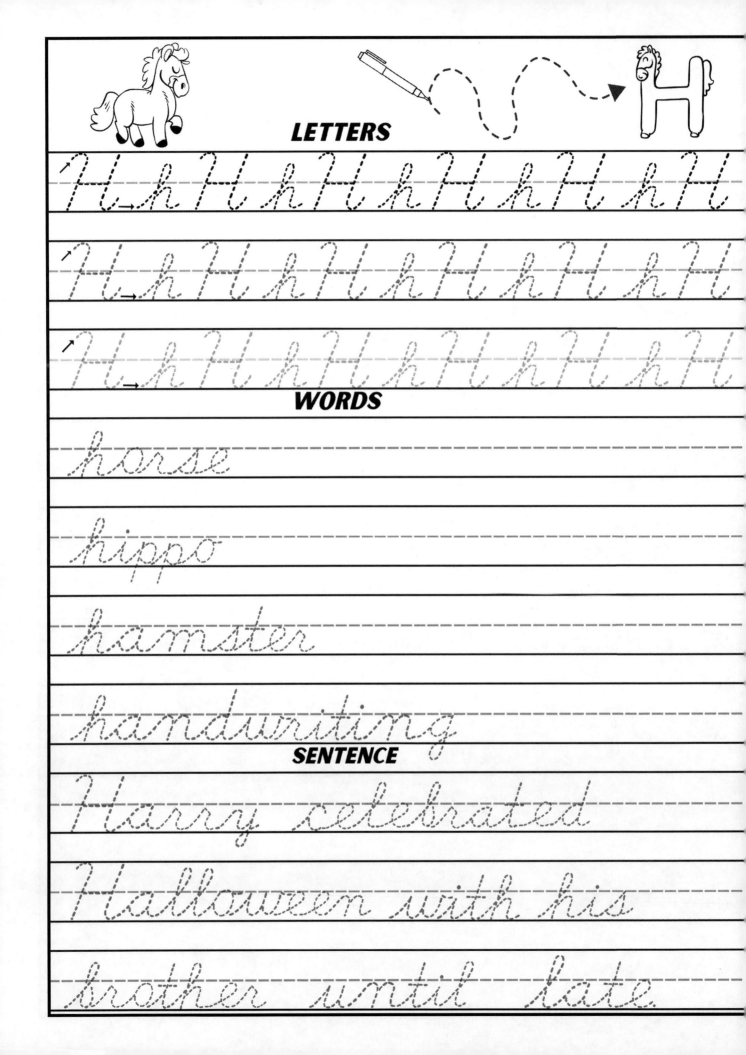

LETTERS

Hh Hh Hh Hh Hh Hh Hh Hh

Hh Hh Hh Hh Hh Hh Hh Hh

Hh Hh Hh Hh Hh Hh Hh Hh

WORDS

horse

hippo

hamster

handwriting

SENTENCE

Harry celebrated

Halloween with his

brother until late

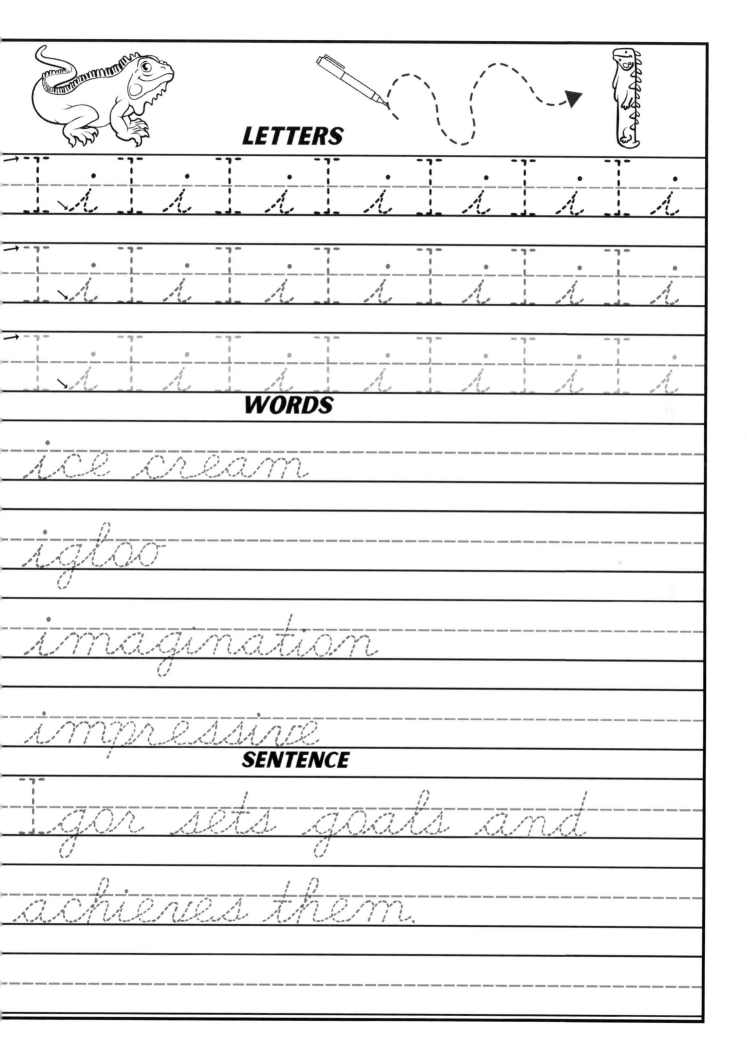

LETTERS

WORDS

ice cream

igloo

imagination

impressive

SENTENCE

Igor sets goals and

achieves them.

J J J J J J J J J J J J J
J J J J J J J J J J J J J
J J J J J J J J J J J J J

jellyfish

jaguar

jacuzzi

joke

Johnny and Jake found

cute jewellery in jungle

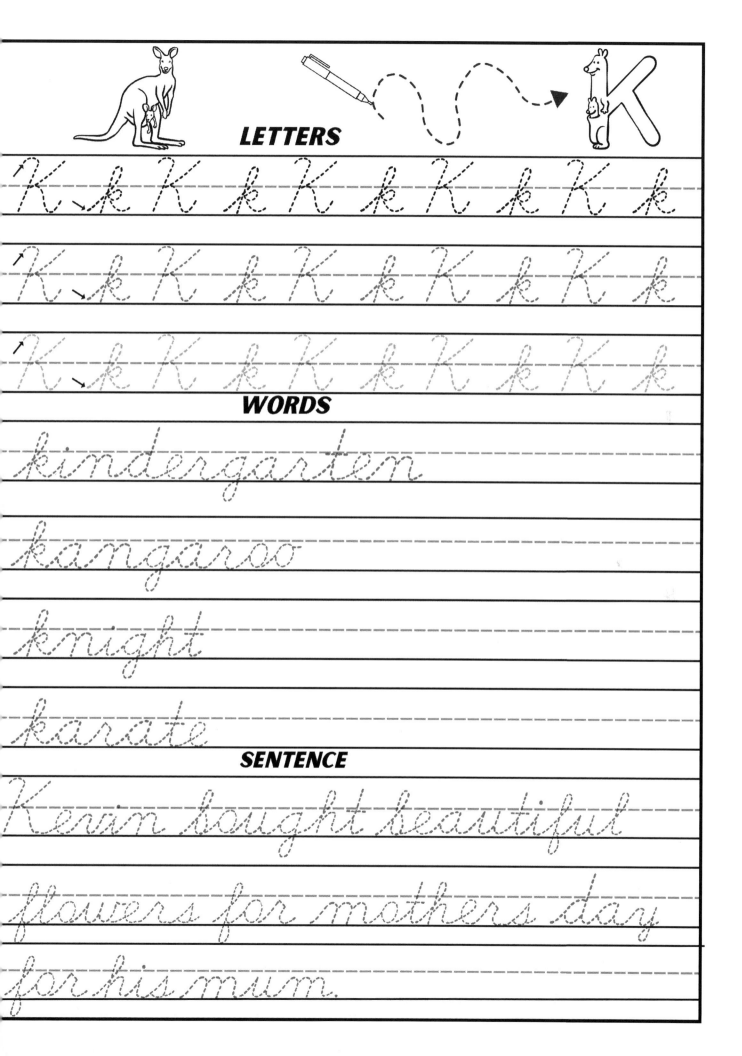

LETTERS

K k k K k K k K k K k K k

K k k K k K k K k K k K k

K k k K k K k K k K k K k

WORDS

kindergarten

kangaroo

knight

karate

SENTENCE

Kevin bought beautiful

flowers for mothers day

for his mum.

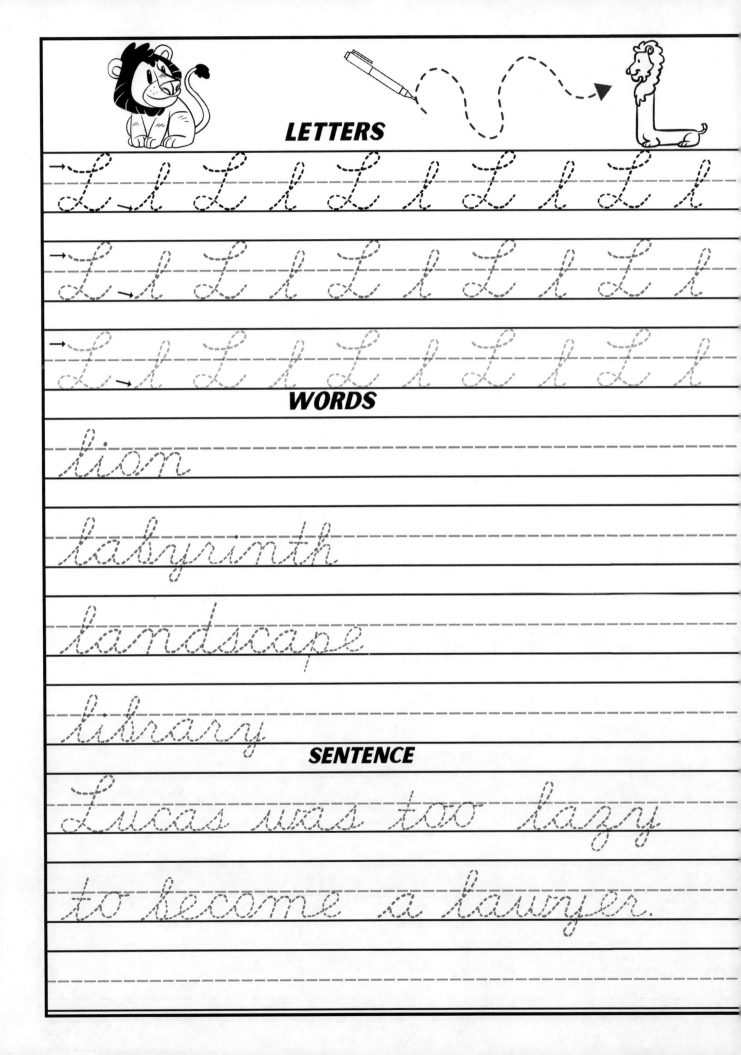

LETTERS

→ ℒ ℓ ℒ ℓ ℒ ℓ ℒ ℓ ℒ ℓ ℒ ℓ

→ ℒ ℓ ℒ ℓ ℒ ℓ ℒ ℓ ℒ ℓ ℒ ℓ

→ ℒ ℓ ℒ ℓ ℒ ℓ ℒ ℓ ℒ ℓ ℒ ℓ

WORDS

lion

labyrinth

landscape

library

SENTENCE

Lucas was too lazy

to become a lawyer.

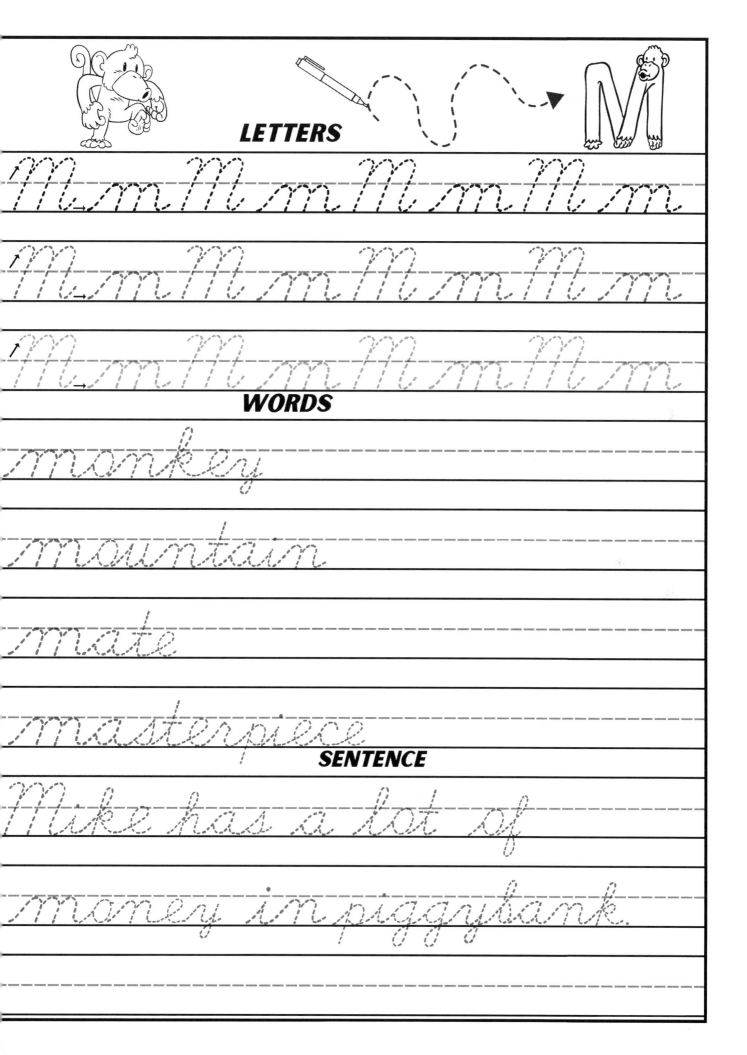

LETTERS

Mm Mm Mm Mm
Mm Mm Mm Mm
Mm Mm Mm Mm

WORDS

monkey

mountain

mate

masterpiece

SENTENCE

Mike has a lot of
money in piggybank.

LETTERS

Nn Nn Nn Nn Nn Nn Nn Nn Nn Nn

Nn Nn Nn Nn Nn Nn Nn Nn Nn Nn

Nn Nn Nn Nn Nn Nn Nn Nn Nn Nn

WORDS

notebook

neighbour

nephew

narwhal

SENTENCE

Nicole and Natalie have

been friends since the

first grade.

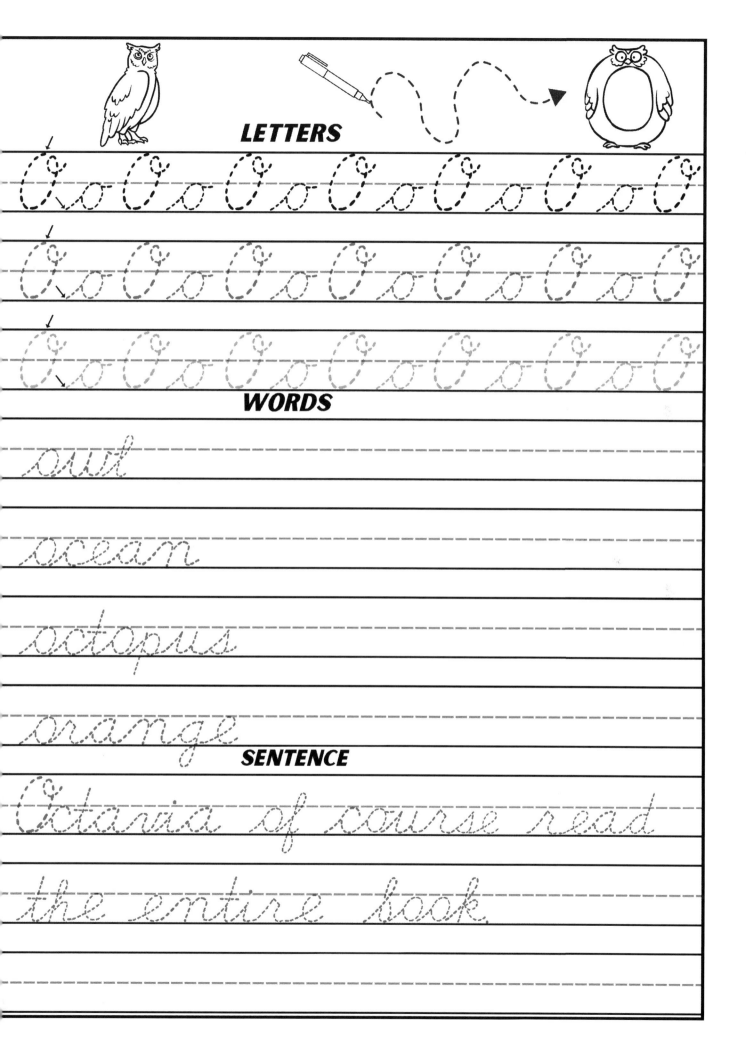

LETTERS

Oo Oo Oo Oo Oo Oo Oo Oo

Oo Oo Oo Oo Oo Oo Oo Oo

Oo Oo Oo Oo Oo Oo Oo Oo

WORDS

out

ocean

octopus

orange

SENTENCE

Octavia of course read

the entire book.

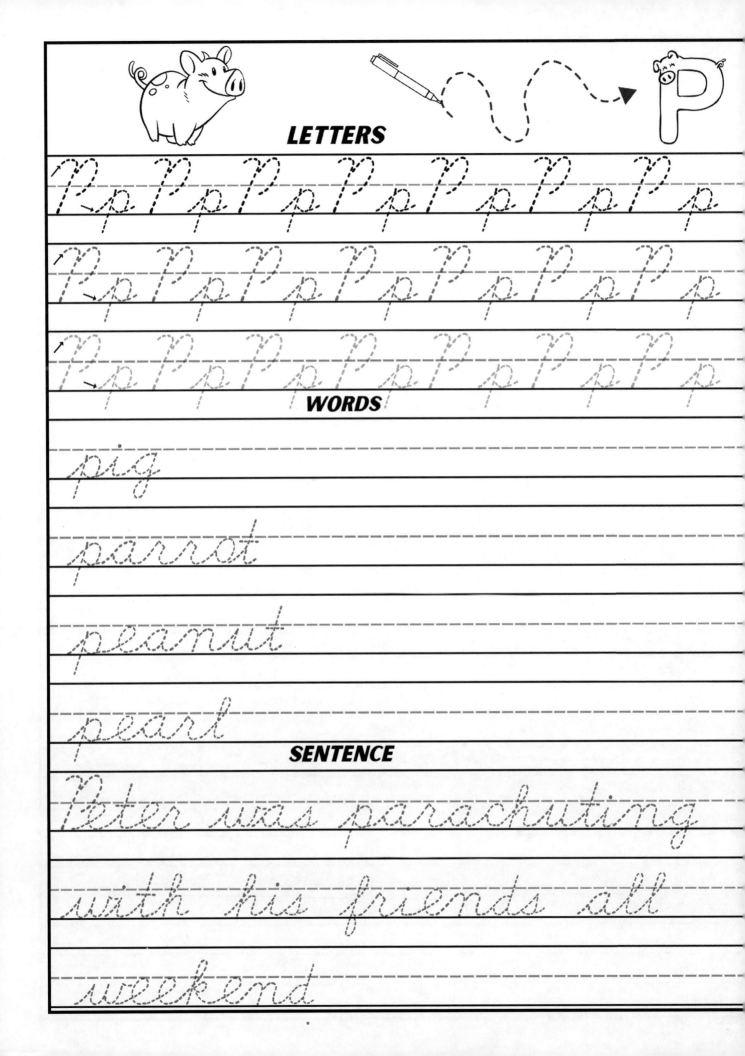

LETTERS

Pp Pp Pp Pp Pp Pp Pp Pp Pp Pp

Pp Pp Pp Pp Pp Pp Pp Pp Pp Pp

Pp Pp Pp Pp Pp Pp Pp Pp Pp Pp

WORDS

pig

parrot

peanut

pearl

SENTENCE

Peter was parachuting

with his friends all

weekend

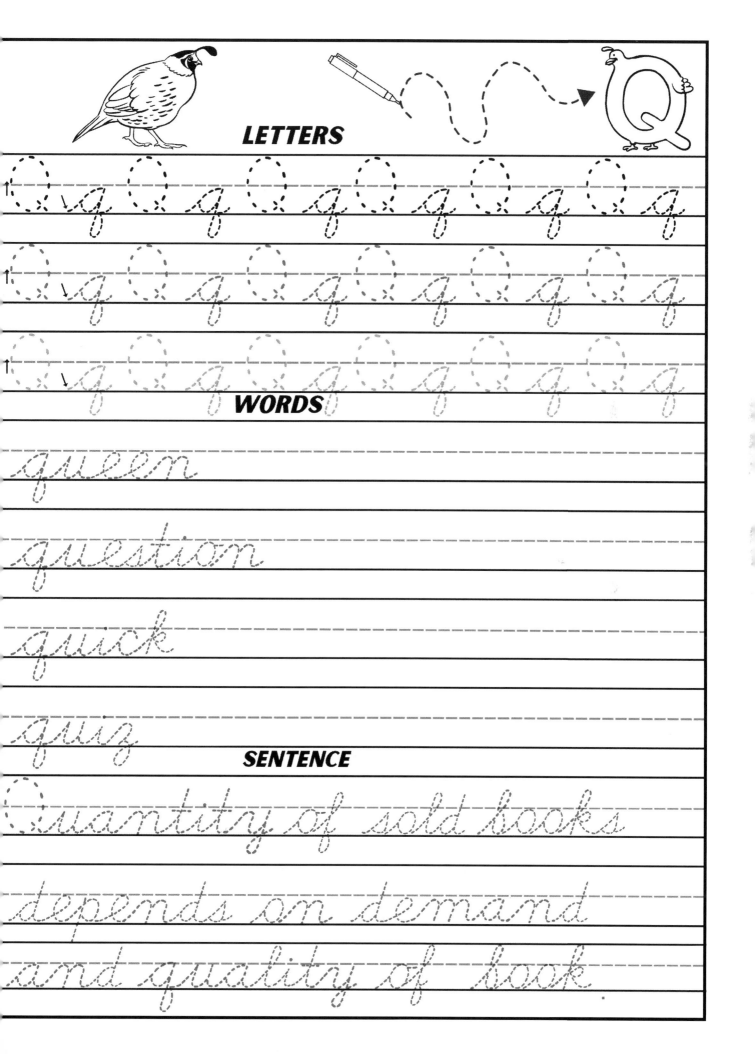

LETTERS

q q q q q q q q q q q

q q q q q q q q q q q

q q q q q q q q q q q

WORDS

queen

question

quick

quiz

SENTENCE

Quantity of sold books

depends on demand

and quality of book

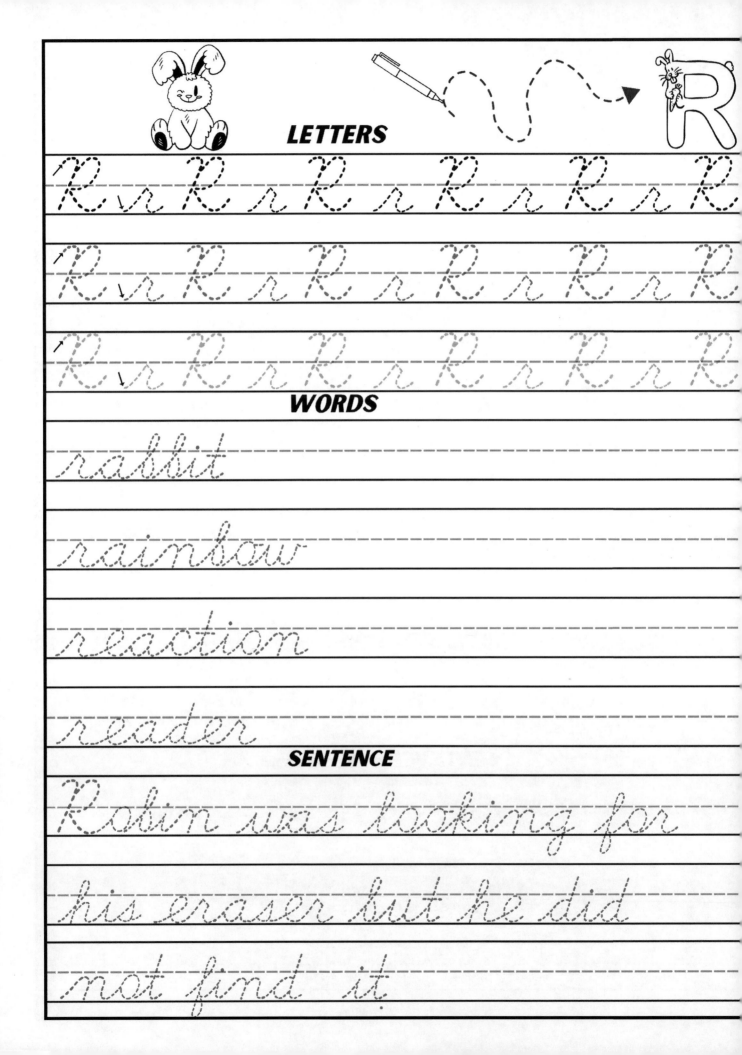

LETTERS

R r R r R r R r R r R r R

R r R r R r R r R r R r R

R r R r R r R r R r R r R

WORDS

rabbit

rainbow

reaction

reader

SENTENCE

Robin was looking for

his eraser but he did

not find it.

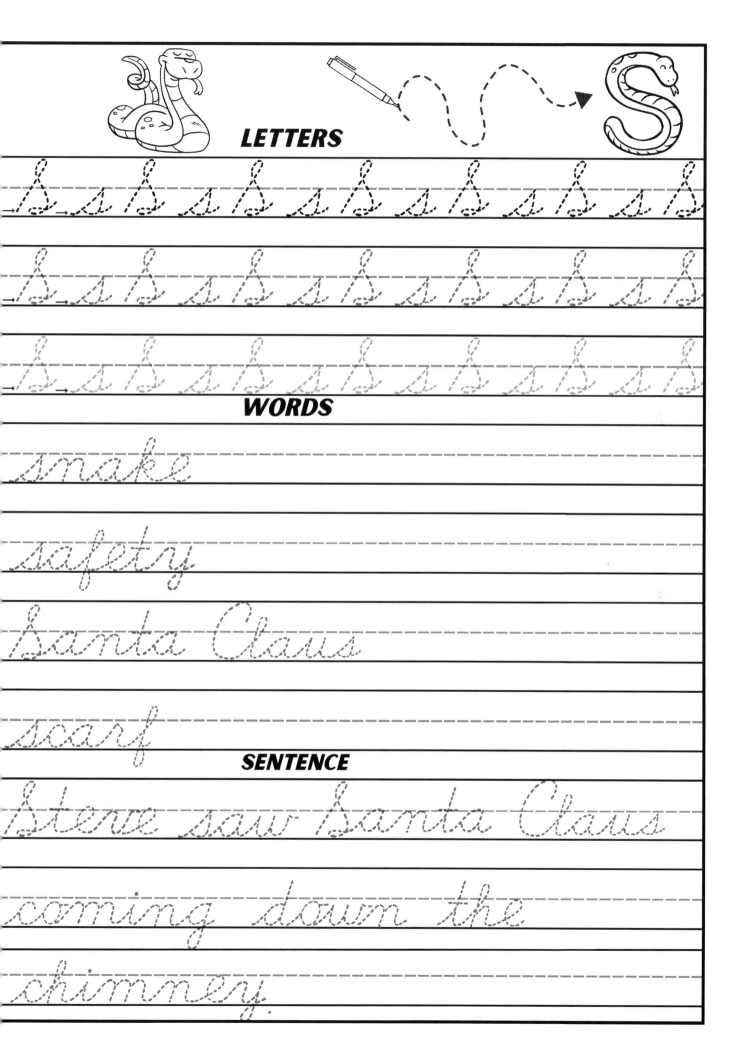

LETTERS

WORDS

snake

safety

Santa Claus

scarf

SENTENCE

Steve saw Santa Claus

coming down the

chimney.

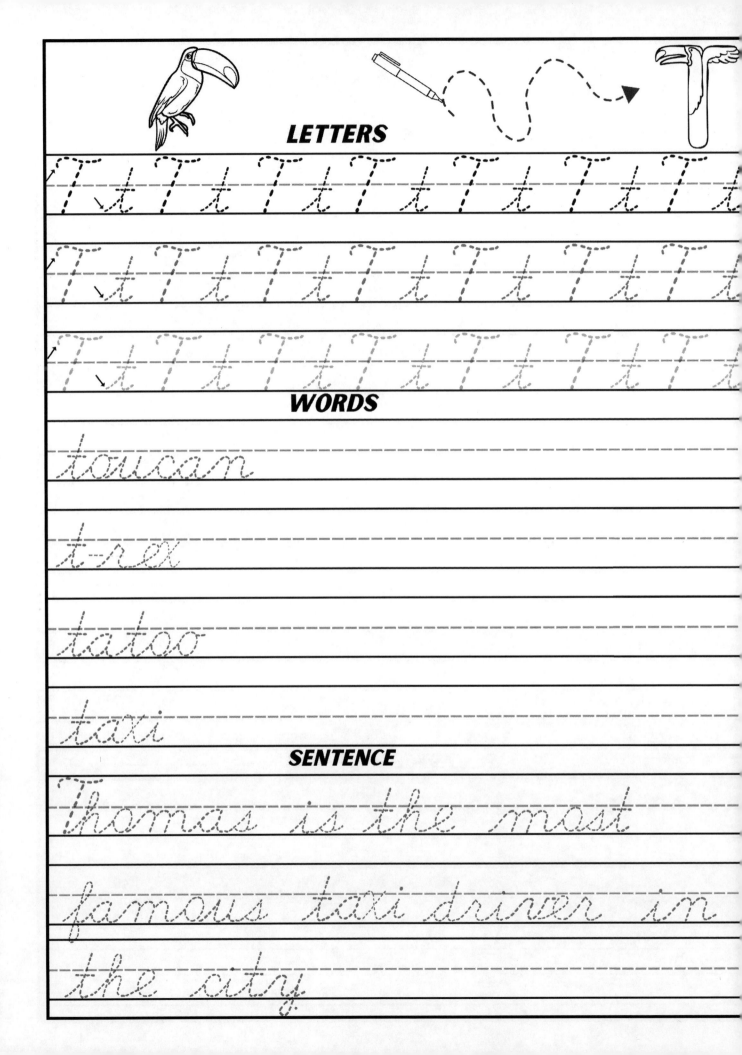

LETTERS

Tt Tt Tt Tt Tt Tt Tt Tt Tt Tt Tt
Tt Tt Tt Tt Tt Tt Tt Tt Tt Tt Tt
Tt Tt Tt Tt Tt Tt Tt Tt Tt Tt Tt

WORDS

toucan

t-rex

tatoo

taxi

SENTENCE

Thomas is the most
famous taxi driver in
the city.

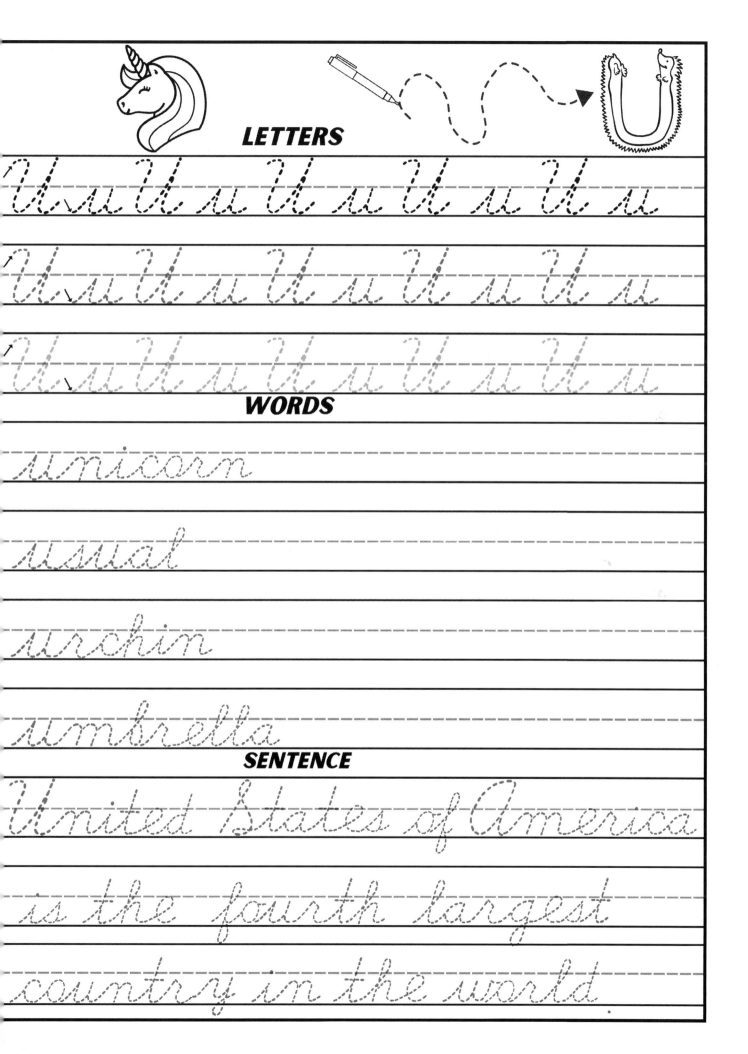

LETTERS

$\mathcal{U}$ u $\mathcal{U}$ u $\mathcal{U}$ u $\mathcal{U}$ u $\mathcal{U}$ u

$\mathcal{U}$ u $\mathcal{U}$ u $\mathcal{U}$ u $\mathcal{U}$ u $\mathcal{U}$ u

$\mathcal{U}$ u $\mathcal{U}$ u $\mathcal{U}$ u $\mathcal{U}$ u $\mathcal{U}$ u

WORDS

unicorn

usual

urchin

umbrella

SENTENCE

United States of America

is the fourth largest

country in the world

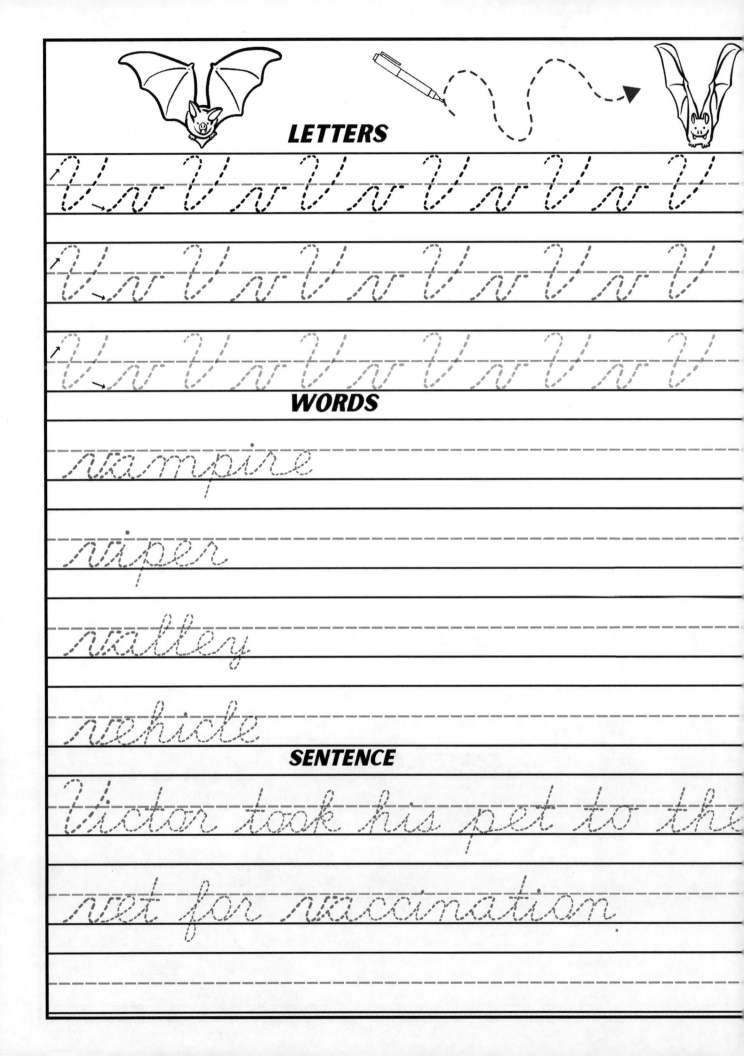

LETTERS

𝒱 𝓋 𝒱 𝓋 𝒱 𝓋 𝒱 𝓋 𝒱 𝓋 𝒱

𝒱 𝓋 𝒱 𝓋 𝒱 𝓋 𝒱 𝓋 𝒱 𝓋 𝒱

𝒱 𝓋 𝒱 𝓋 𝒱 𝓋 𝒱 𝓋 𝒱 𝓋 𝒱

WORDS

vampire

viper

valley

vehicle

SENTENCE

Victor took his pet to the

vet for vaccination.

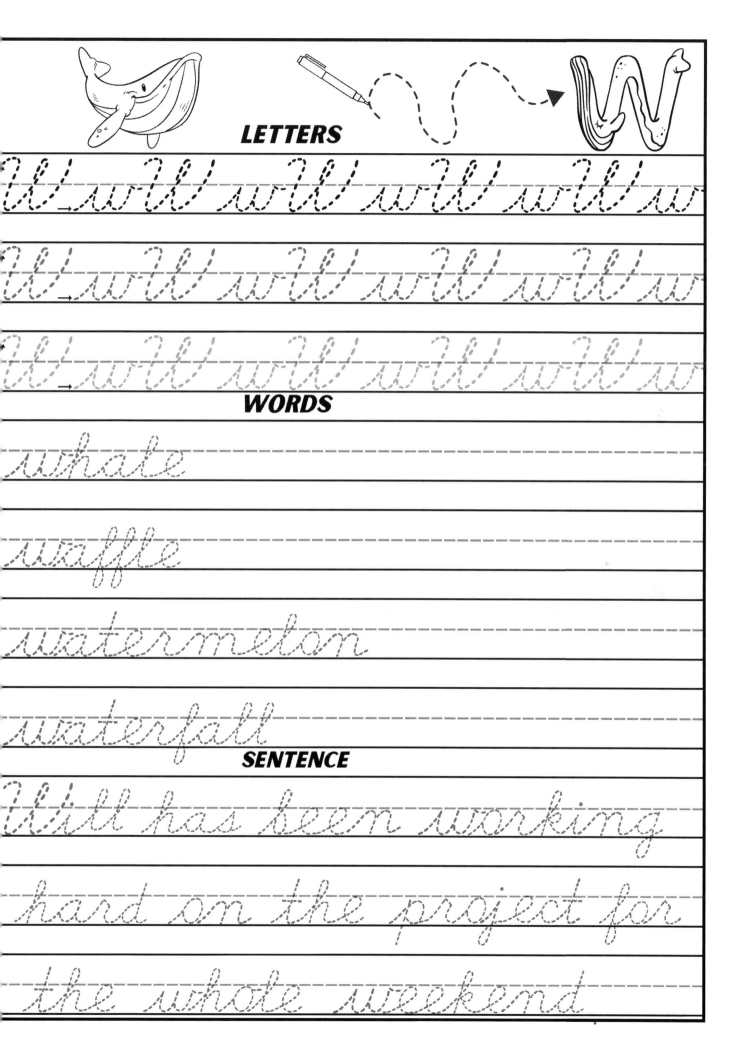

LETTERS

𝒲 w𝒲 w𝒲 w𝒲 w𝒲 w

𝒲 w𝒲 w𝒲 w𝒲 w𝒲 w

𝒲 w𝒲 w𝒲 w𝒲 w𝒲 w

WORDS

whale

waffle

watermelon

waterfall

SENTENCE

Will has been working

hard on the project for

the whole weekend

LETTERS

Yy Yy Yy Yy Yy Yy Yy Yy Yy Yy

Yy Yy Yy Yy Yy Yy Yy Yy Yy Yy

Yy Yy Yy Yy Yy Yy Yy Yy Yy Yy

WORDS

yak

yacht

yoga

yoghurt

SENTENCE

Yasmine is one year

younger than her

sister Youita.

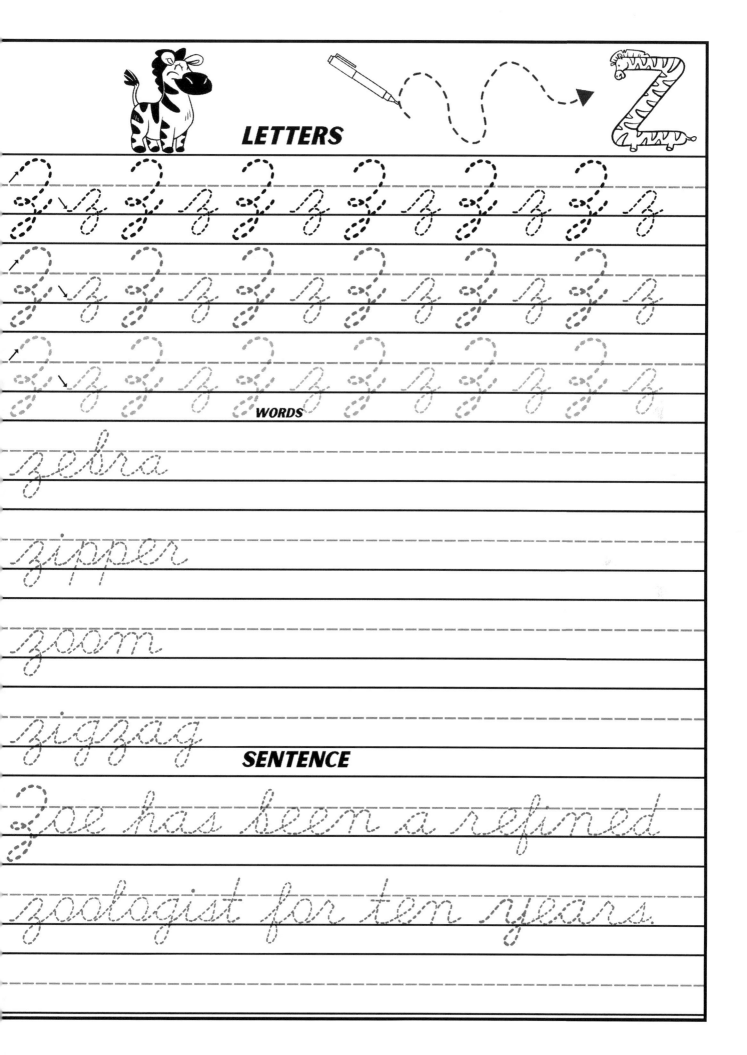

LETTERS

WORDS

zebra

zipper

zoom

zigzag

SENTENCE

Zoe has been a refined

zoologist for ten years.

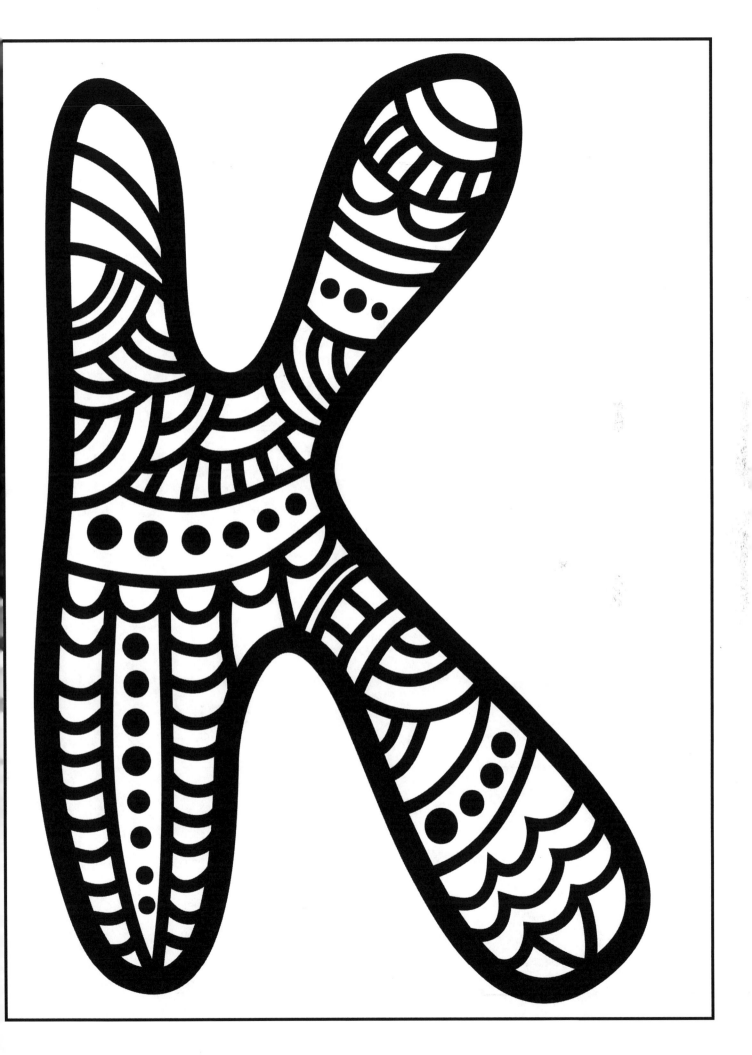

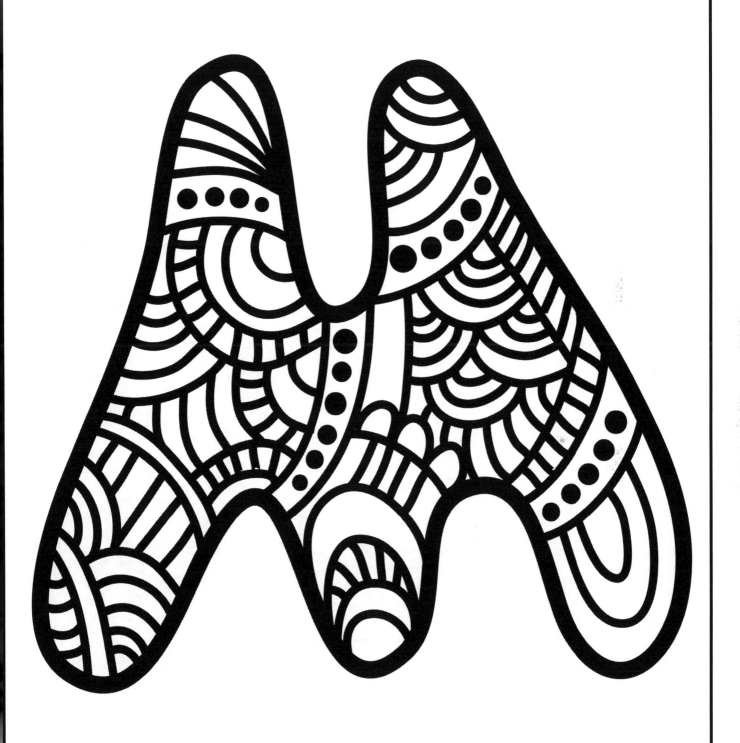

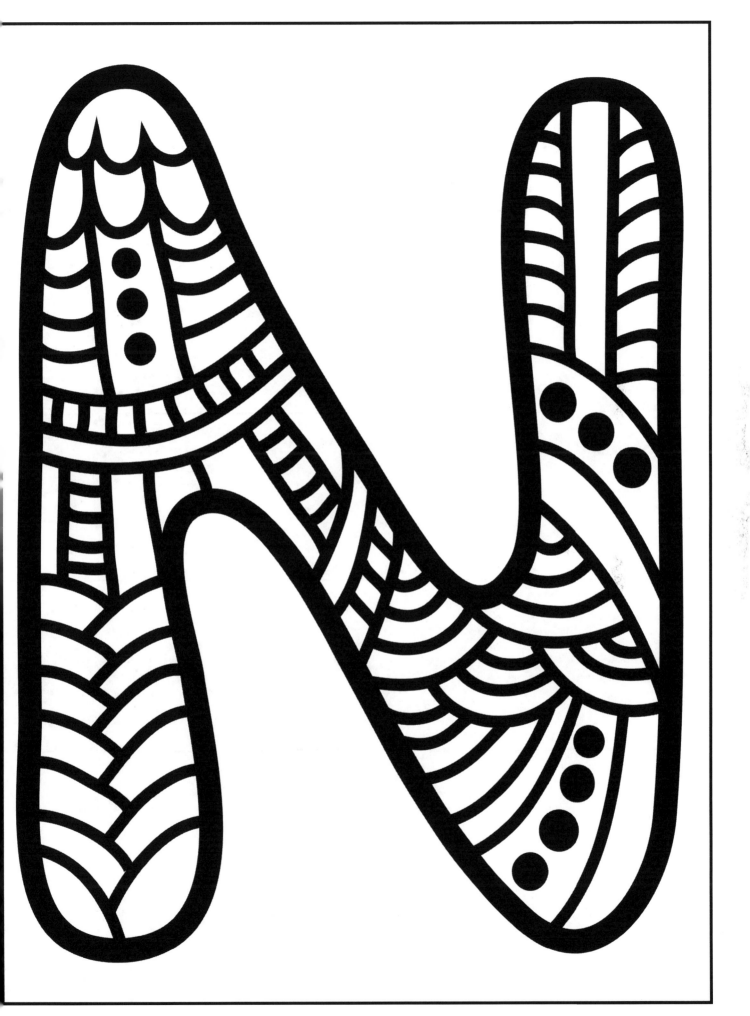

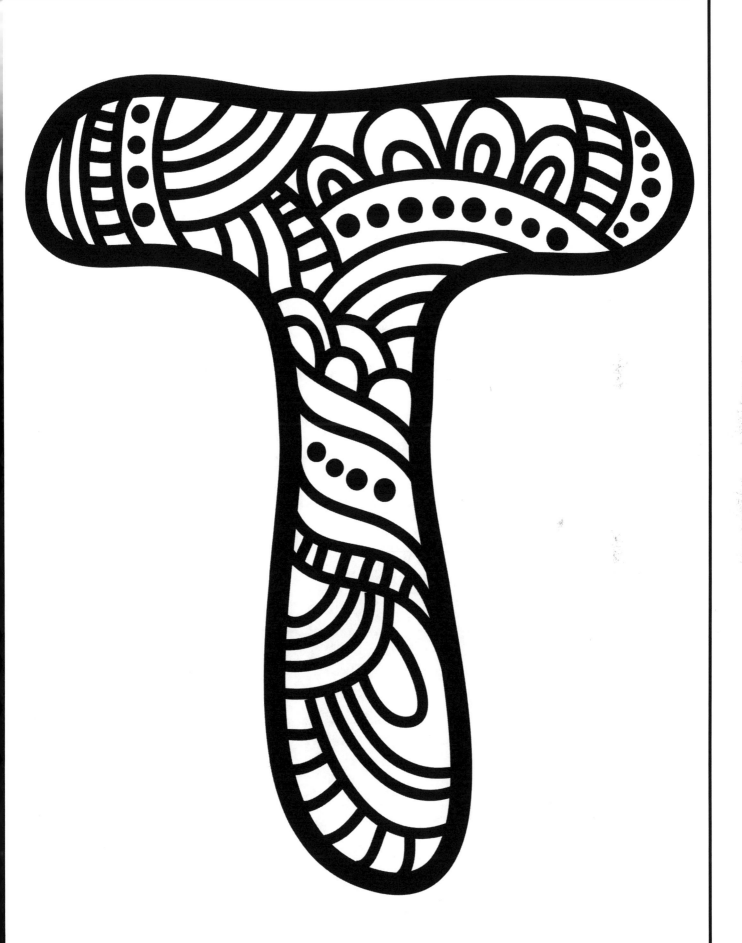

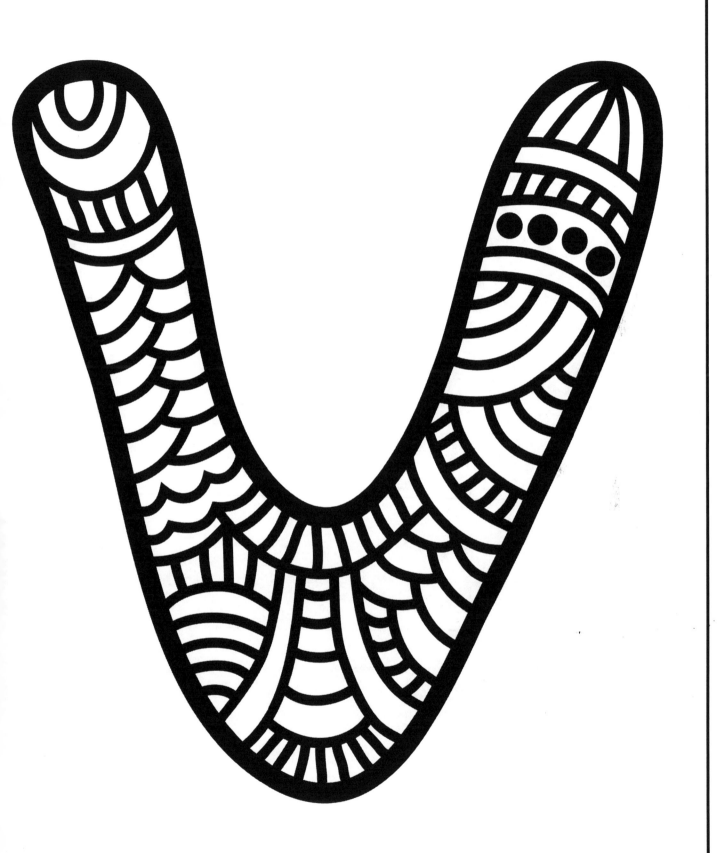

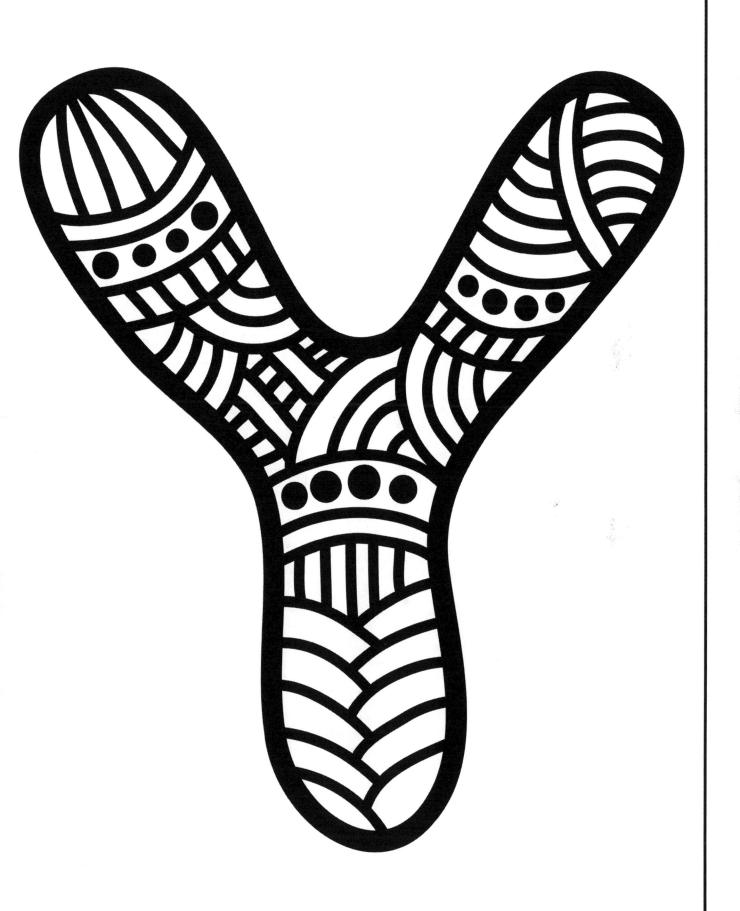

Made in the USA
Columbia, SC
14 December 2024

49288696R00046